I0492601

The Great Reset
Hidden Agenda

By Blu Diamond

The Great Reset Hidden Agenda Copyright © 2021
by Blu Diamond All Rights Reserved.
No part of this book may be used or reproduced in any
manner without prior written permission from the publisher,
except in the case of brief quotations embodied in critical
reviews and articles.
The scanning, uploading, and distribution of this text via the
Internet or via any other means without the permission of the
publisher is illegal and punishable by law. Please purchase
only authorized electronic editions, and do not participate in
or encourage electronic piracy of copyrighted materials.

Your support of the author's rights is appreciated. Cover
designed by Blu Diamond
Visit my author website at www.bludiamond.org
Visit my website and blog page at www.universalmizfitz.com
Printed in the United States of America First Printing: March
2021
Universal Mizfitz Publishing Inc.
P.O. Box 377
Philo, Oh. 43771

ISBN- 9798717348478

Dedication

I want to dedicate this book to the hard-working men and women of our society. I want you to remember that there are always two sides to every story. Yes, it is true that we need to confront the damage that has been done to the Earth and clean up our mess, but we should not have to go to war and destroy everything in our path. Have we not grown up at all? What everyone needs to know, is that if we plan on crossing over into the next phase, we have to get this right. This is a real live test of what we have learned until now. We better get it right!

Table of Contents

Preface

This Great Reset can go really good or really bad. The one thing that I can guarantee to you is as they chose to move forward with these technological advancements then the working class better get caught up to speed quickly so we can keep a very close eye on how these advancements are rolled out.

In this situation I can see both sides of this coin. Because of my training I can also see where the elite will be defeated if they took the real mark that God marked on Satan. Let me show you how they will be defeated!

Chapter 1
Covid19 the Perfect Storm

When I was a child my grandfather used to tell me that there was a group of people who managed all of the resources that the working class depended on to survive. Honestly, at the time I had figured that he was exaggerating. I had a hard time wrapping my head around the fact that a small group could have that kind of influence on an entire planet of people.

Now, with the recent developments of a global pandemic and our current age of information technology we can see how these global systems are struggling to continue to function in order to support the countries that are in dire need of assistance. Let me just say right here, I can see both sides of this equation. In the first part of this short book, I will lay out both sides, so that you can see the whole scene, then we will go into how these groups are being led to the slaughter by an ancient hidden agenda.

Many of us around the world have suddenly been made aware of these global management systems that have been put in place. This is known as the "supply chain." Ironically, they really have not existed for hundreds of years like you might think.

For example, the United Nations is an international organization founded in 1945 in the United States after World War II by fifty-one countries that were committed to maintaining international peace and security in an effort to develop friendly relations among nations and promoting social progress, better living standards and human rights. Underline 'in an effort.' When you look back on their success, in the grand scheme of things they have been successful in avoiding another World War. Even though "smaller" wars have broken out, there has not been one that is considered a World War.

The organization that the entire planet is paying close attention to during this pandemic is a group called the World Economic Forum. It was established in 1971 as a not-for-profit foundation headquartered in Geneva, Switzerland that engages the foremost political, business, cultural and other leaders of society to shape global, regional and industry agendas. This one is the one to watch closely because they are made up of the major corporate leaders that trade on a global scale. They meet once a year in January to discuss their projections and plans for the coming year. This year in 2021 was the first time that they actually gave the public an "inside" peek at what these discussions look like, in my opinion, could be a good thing if we use this information right, and obviously have pushed some people over the edge.

There is one more group that plays a huge part in this and that is called the World Trade Organization. This is a bit different because this one began initially by establishing a Tariff and Trade Agreement in 1948 between countries in an effort for the United Nations to help create a system that helps established countries who create products to sell and trade with other countries in order for that country to flourish.

This system has worked very well in helping third world countries begin to look at how to form companies that can produce what is called a "Gross Domestic Product" for their country. When a country can create a product that other countries need, then that country's economy will begin to flourish, as we have seen in countries like Venezuela over the years.

As you can imagine, all of these systems only work if the working class is able to report to work to manufacture their country's Gross Domestic Product (GDP).

So, when Covid19 hit, and these countries had to shut down production, it has caused a ripple effect throughout these systems. As you probably could imagine, even after the workers could go back to work, other countries were fearful of trading products from hot zones. That creates an even greater problem for these countries' economies. After all, when the Chinese government eased the shut down and had their people go back to working their production lines, very few countries were willing to accept anything being shipped out of there. Do you blame them?

The global financial institutions are struggling to figure out a way to keep the whole world from going into a Great Depression, at the same time that we are still dealing with this virus. So, what I want you to see is that this is not one group against the working class. Even though these groups work together in such a way to sustain a quality of life for everyone involved, it is true that the leaders of

these corporations have a much better quality of life then their workers.

The thing that is different about this particular time is that the founder of the World Economic Forum, Klaus Schwab is introducing two options to these global leaders. These two options are centered around the real issue that humanity is facing with the climate change that is happening on the planet. This is why Klaus is saying that Capitalism is dead. What he is referring to is that the previous ways that corporate shareholders have been only focused on profits and not the impact of their actions been on society and the environment is dead. We can no longer turn a blind eye to the selfishness and greed. As you watch this unfold you will see that this is not one group against humanity, but these actions will flush out the hidden agenda and who is pushing it from behind the curtain.

Whether you believe in the climate change or not, what I want to show you in this book is that we have a window of opportunity to act in order to effectively reverse the damage that many corporations have done to the Earth and ecosystems across the globe.

I commend Mr. Schwab for taking on these world leaders to hold them accountable using peer pressure to clean up their act and repair the damage. That part of this agenda appears as a "noble cause." And these people know him, he is the founder of this organization and they have all been doing business together for a long time. His approach is ingenious in one way that it gives these groups that understand money and economic systems a tangible technique to see how their corporations impact the Earth and make them accountable for replenishing it instead of leaving destruction in their wake based only on greed. He has set up a system of energy credits to earn, spend or save. This will give these global corporations incentives to hit specific climate impact goals, hopefully it will work.

The thing that does not make sense to many of the working class, is why it is necessary for these global corporations to shift their labor force to robotics and autonomy and eliminate jobs in the midst of a global economic emergency. Or why the elite are buying up farmland and getting into farming to put the small farmers out of business. Which also sets up a situation where the masses will have to depend on one group to feed themselves and their families. Sounds like the mark of the beast now doesn't it?

As these supply chains become more automated, there are going to be massive amounts of people put out of work in a short amount of time. And because this is a shift in the corporate sector, most governments that are set up as a Democracy cannot dictate to any private or publicly traded company to maintain their workers or not. And these governments cannot dictate how these corporations spend or invest their money. Many of these corporations are run by their shareholders. And we all know that the only thing shareholders are interested in is maximizing their profit margins. It appears to me that the next war that will show up soon is going to be a war of these corporations against each other with the working class caught in the middle.

We are already seeing this taking place in some cities across the United States. Klaus calls this the

4th Industrial Revolution. I can see in one way how that would be beneficial to a country that is dealing with a virus when their workers cannot report to work, then by using autonomy in the corporations that produce products that are traded on an international scale, they would still be able to produce their product and because it has not been touched by human hands other countries would not be fearful to purchase that product.

So, his system can possibly fix that situation, although it would not put the whole country out of work. It will require reeducating the working class to learn new skills and trades. For some that will be easy, for others it will be nearly an impossible task. And as you can see from our current governments the working class cannot depend on them to be consistent in helping to sustain us. The writing is on the wall. Absolute power corrupts absolutely.

This is why you will be seeing how this forum is suggesting that we will not own anything in the future, and we will be "happy." I know that does not sound like paradise to you, the thought of not having ownership, but I want you to take a good look around your city. How many homeless have been created because of this perfect storm? When someone does not have what they need to survive or feed themselves or their children, they turn to criminal activity to do whatever it takes.

Poverty has been the underlying problem in our society that causes all crime. In my opinion, the worse part of that problem is how I have seen all good people turn their heads each day at another person in need and they walk away so satisfied thinking that the person in need must be an addict or an alcoholic, when the real reason a person will turn to these vices to deal with life is because they have fallen in the cracks of our society and because they don't have an address or can't afford a cell phone. No employer will take a chance and give someone a job to help them out if they do not have an address or phone number to put on the application. They become trapped this is the real reason that once you lose your job and cannot get another one, then it is a domino effect throughout every part of your life quickly. Do you see the storm on the horizon yet? It is coming to the middle class as well.

Now as you sit in your pretty home, I want to show you what has been happening in Hollywood California during this pandemic. I will not mention the real names of the people that this situation happened to, because of their celebrity status, but this is just one case that took place.

A well to do couple that lived in a nice big house, had a confrontation that shocked them into reality. The wife had opened up her living room windows to let in the beautiful sunshine and fresh air, when she noticed a group of vagrants that were sitting on their retaining wall near their front security gate. She yelled out to them, "You better leave before I call the police!" The vagrants waived a gun and replied, "Go ahead!" Just before this pandemic there has been a mass exodus from well to do areas. During the summer and fall of last year there was an even greater number of people who moved out of major cities.

Currently in most states police will not respond unless there is a life-threatening situation. I had a friend of mine in Ohio that was held up at gun point and robbed just after his wife's death. Because he had a back injury and could not take care of his home himself, he had hired a cleaning lady. She is the one who orchestrated the home invasion. This took place two years before this pandemic and the police simply took his statement and did nothing. The police have taken a lot of bad publicity. Would you want their job? As this 4th Industrial Revolution continues to march forward the amount of people who will be displaced is going to skyrocket. They will be outnumbered easily. Most Police do not make much money for the amount of risk in the job. How long do you think these people will stay on the job if it gets really bad? Do you think that there will be new applicants to recruit as this agenda hits our country? No one will sign up for that job and put their life into danger. That would be a suicide mission. Very few people have that kind of dedication to serving the public who hates them.

I am here to tell you, if you think you will be safe in your home when more than half of the workforce goes homeless, you have got another thing coming! And to make matters worse our social services are not set up to handle massive amounts of people losing their jobs and going hungry. Our homeless shelters and food banks are set up only on donations of charity, this when you will be in for a rude awakening of Biblical proportions! This is why Jesus said in Mathew 6:19 "Lay not up for yourselves treasures upon the earth, where moth and rust do corrupt and where thieves break through and steal."

In January 2021, the Los Angeles times reported that a U.S. Census found that 1.9 million adult Californians reported being behind on their rent. That is not including utilities, let alone paying for internet to work from home or home school their children. Now, do you think that these people are able to afford food? Remember the long lines at the food banks during this pandemic?

This is a systemic human emergency across every country right now! This is the humanitarian efforts that require these global corporations to infuse our society with money and resources as soon as humanly possible. If not, there will not be any safe place to go when humanity becomes desperate to survive.

This is the real reason why Klaus is saying that no one will own anything. Because at the point that the people who "have resources" are keeping it to themselves they become the target of aggression. I can see this problem from both sides of the fence.

Chapter 2
While You Were Sleeping

What I want to show you, in this section, is the real reason that this virus had to happen and how these types of events prevent us as a human race from destroying ourselves until we figure out how to confront this issue and take personal responsibility for our part in creating this mess. Because I want you to see that every class of our society has contributed to these problems that we will now have to face together.

If you live on a large continent you may think that this problem does not affect you. I am going to show you how it really does and if you do not face it now it will consume your children, and this is the real reason that the generation that came after the Millennial Generation is known as Generation Z. Because if we ignore this now then that will be the last generation.

From 1800 to 1927 it took 127 years for the Earth's human population to double from one billion to two billion. Then it took only 47 years from 1927 to 1974 to double from two billion to four billion. Since 1960, the world population has grown by about one billion every 13 years! That breaks down to approximately 200,000 new babies that are born each day to add to this figure. That is about 140 additional people per minute!

Now let us look at this from what these people's job has been on the planet, at what number would you sound the alarm that we have a problem here? How can these global leaders tell any country to put restrictions on how many children a family can have, and would their government actually enforce

it? Would their society comply? This has already been a major issue in some countries like China (previous page) and India (above).

Look at it like this, the more children that we have, the more jobs we have to create to feed them, which leads to building more corporations to create jobs and building more housing to house them. All of which require more land being taken away from our ecosystems and farming to feed them. And the bottom line that these overpopulated countries have realized is that there is only so much land to go around.

Most of our building materials come from Earth based products harvested from trees and so on. Now think about this, do you know how many trees it takes to provide toilet paper for that amount of people? During the beginning of the pandemic there was a rush on toilet paper purchasing which caused a shortage. What the public did not see on the news is how many trees had to be mass cut to produce more for the masses! Here are the hard cold facts, 27,000 trees are cut each DAY for toilet paper production. It takes a tree 20 years to get to maturity to be used for paper products, not to mention all of the other building materials that we use wood for, from our houses, our decks, our cabinetry, our furniture and so on.

We currently have the technology to make paper products from bamboo which grows to maturity faster and requires less water and is a renewable resource that is sustainable. This is just one area that we harvest trees for our everyday products. Not to mention paper towels, napkins, notebook paper, copy paper and so on. This is the real reason that the Earth's forests are being destroyed quickly. This alone will destroy eco systems including all wildlife. Without trees to filter the air we are painting ourselves into a corner for an epic systemic failure, across this planet!

My point is this, when will we take personal responsibility for what we use, how our companies package their products, how we dispose of these products when we are finished and revamping our trash processing system!

Our oceans are polluted, our landfills are full of products that will NEVER biodegrade. That does not even take a look at the last thirty years of the computer age and how many of these "toys" are disposed of and where are they now? There are tech landfills that are polluting the planet with chemicals that were never an issue in human history before now. These tech companies need to be involved in planning ways to dispose of these products when they break, or we are forced to upgrade. Honestly, what is the plan here people? Why have we not instituted laws to mandate the disposal of a product before rolling out the newest invention?

If we continue to hit the "snooze bar" and ignore the problem we will seal our own fate in so many ways as a human race, that we will never dig our way out! This is the real reason that we all must join this conversation that the elite are having, in order to make sure that every class of society can have a voice in these changes and help make this transition safely for all.

Currently they are looking to change the way we produce food for the nations because they are estimating that we need to feed 12 billion within the next 8 years! Then we have less time than that to deal with feeding twice that!

I am willing to bet that at some point we might find that someone will discover that the S.A.R.S. types of viruses have a side effect of sterility. Since 2016 there has been a rapid decline in child births and an increase in sterility cases. As a simple mathematical equation on average one in three people would get a virus. These strains have minimal symptoms and hit the childbearing age group. The sick and elderly will die off from them. And it is a way that they could approach a solution to this dire situation that no one knows how to solve. That solution was revealed in Dan Brown's book 'Inferno' in 2013. Did he know something that the rest of the world was clueless to at the time?

We have been getting subtle warning signs over the years that these issues are real, and yet most people continued to brush it under the rug and ignore it. Now you hear people like Elon Musk giving his, "Last Warning" on it last Tuesday February 16, 2021 on CNN Money. His "Last Warning" was that we needed to stop having babies and yet he has 6 kids. I am here to tell you, that this virus was just the 'warning shot' above our heads. This gave our countries the warning and preparation time to get everything in place. The next one will be much more lethal. Just like the 1900's. The elite rolled out a plan for another Industrial Revolution, then suddenly there was a pandemic that killed off a large portion of the working class. Then in order to kickstart the global economies they needed a world war. Which is what the Bible says will be coming up soon.

This is the real reason that we must deal with restricting meat consumption. When farmers are faced with not being able to keep up with the demand for food and they have to resort to genetically modifying seeds to guarantee high yielding crops or resorting to growth hormones to make their livestock mature faster to harvest them, then we have a major problem!

When we are looking to feed 12 billion meat eaters on the planet, how is that going to work? Currently our oceans are divided up into fishing lanes. Each country is given a specific time to harvest the marine life. Some cultures depend more on marine life than others.

We need to change our eating habits. We all know how difficult it can be when you start a new diet to change the way you are used to eating and how often we eat. Look at the different cultures in the different countries and their religious traditions.

These traditions are usually based on certain foods as a central part of the celebration.

Marine life is a delicate eco system most of which cannot be duplicated on land or in a lab. These cultures are mainly landlocked countries that are running out of real estate for food production. Now they are actively buying up land in other countries. If you view this as a threat to your country, then you are setting yourself up for a similar problem because they will do what they have to in order to feed their working class. This is why we are looking at other possibilities and urging people to eat more plant-based diets.

Also, it is Biblical! We were never supposed to eat the meat of anything that had blood in it. We have gone astray from that plan as a culture and if we would have maintained that then our eco systems would be in better condition now. But hindsight is always 20/20! No pun intended.

The Great Reset Hidden Agenda

Chapter 3
Seeing Through the Veil of Your 'Enemy'

Many Christians have drawn the conclusion throughout history that in the 'End Times' that there will be a false prophet that forms a one world government.

In the book of Revelation chapter 13, in Apostle John's vision he sees the "beast" rising out of the sea having seven heads and ten horns. Most people combine this vision with Daniel's vision that is similar, many have drawn the conclusion that some sort of world system will be inaugurated by the beast, the most powerful "horn" who will defeat the other nine and will begin to wage war against Christians.

This ten-nation confederacy is also seen in the image of the statue in Daniel 2:41-42 where he pictures the final world government consisting of ten entities represented by ten toes of the statue. The scriptures are clear that the beast will either destroy them or reduce their power to nothing more than figureheads. In the end, will they do his bidding?

Later in this book I will show you exactly how they will be destroyed, if these elite took the real mark of that beast.

Apostle John goes on to describe the ruler of this vast empire as having power and great authority, given to him by Satan himself. In Revelations 13:2-4 this man was followed by and even receiving worship from "all of the world and having authority over every tribe, people, language and nation"

From this description many have assumed that this person is the leader of a one-world government which is recognized as sovereign over all other governments.

Once entrenched in power, the beast (Anti-Christ) and the power behind him (Satan) will move to establish absolute control over all people of the Earth to accomplish their true end, the worship that Satan has been seeking ever since being thrown out of Heaven.

In Revelations 13:16-17 it describes one way they will accomplish this by controlling all commerce, and this is where the idea of a one-world currency comes in. These verses go into a description of some sort of satanic mark which will be required in order to buy and sell. This means anyone who refuses the mark will be unable to buy food, clothing, or other necessities of life. In verse 16 it makes it clear that this will be a universal system of control where everyone, rich and poor, great, and small, will bear the mark on their hand or forehead. With current technology it is not much of a stretch of the imagination that this is completely within the realm of possibilities today.

There have even been discussions from the tech giants that our future cell phones will be an implant in our hands, and we would not need a separate device. Looking at this Davos agenda it certainly looks like that is how these groups are shaping the world, what do you think?

Many believers are under the impression that the elite are not aware of the End Times Prophesies. From where I sit, I can tell you that most of the time Satanists know the scriptures better than most Christians who go to church every week and 'listen' to the man behind the pulpit give his interpretation to them. It is a proven fact that less than 19% of Christians have read the Bible. Some people do not know that these groups are operating on a specific timeline. They are following these scriptures to the letter. These things are not randomly taking place right now. Everything throughout time has a specific time and place that these things must happen. These things are not easy to go through, but there are specific dates that everything must happen by.

Much like in nature there is a season to everything on the planet. The timeline that these things must take place in is dictated by the anniversary that is coming up quickly! April 9, 2033 will be 2000-year anniversary of the Resurrection. There are two phases of the Tribulation in the Bible, the first phase is considered milder out of the two. The first phase lasts three and a half years, then the Great Tribulation is kicked off and it is brutal! That is triggered by the Great Famine. I believe that they will implement this agenda of the mark of the beast during the second phase of the Tribulation.

I will say this, that these things are being put into place quickly enough that these groups could have most of this system in place by the end of this year. That is to say that these systems behind the scenes will probably be put into place by the end of 2021. On the World Economic Forum website these corporations are planning on taking over the food production and distribution systems across the globe.

This is what the elite are not telling anyone about their Great Reset. Although most believers see it coming. There is an ancient agenda being carried out by many groups of people across the planet. It is like a game of Dominos. Half of the elite are betting that the second coming will not happen, the other half are banking on it, after all they are natural born gamblers.

We can see by watching these global leaders in Davos discussing their agenda for this year 2021, the technology is not up to speed as much as they would like for it to be in order to initiate it now. Honestly, this is how you can tell that the release of this virus was an accident, or as I see it as divine intervention.

This is probably the reason for targets being set out a little bit. As many of us know Artificial Intelligence is not as advanced as they would need in order to carry out this one world domination at the current moment. Man plans his ways, but God directs his steps.

That would mean that there would have to be some really catastrophic events planned in the next five years to pull off the leaders of these countries, some of whom have been sworn enemies since longer than anyone can remember to come together on common ground and submit to the authority of these global leaders. It would literally take an act of God for a few of these groups to work together.

By Blu Diamond

Chapter 4
Practical Strategies to Handle a Bully

L et us begin to peel back the veil of this agenda. You will notice in your own life that if you have a problem that you are not dealing with, it will get bigger and bigger, then one day the situation explodes in your face and you have to deal with it. I have learned in my own life that when God is shining a light on a situation for me to handle, I am quick to confront the issue and go right through the middle of the problem. The reason why is that I know from my own experiences that It takes less time to deal with it if I handle it right when God first shows me that there is an issue coming. I normally find that He gets my attention the first time because He has lined up other situations that will make it easier for me to handle it right then.

Because in this world everything happens in God's perfect timing, no one else.

Whether or not you look at this situation as the glass is half full or half empty, I want to point out a few things that seem minor in our everyday lives that reveal the fact that you are being trained for this epic battle of good against evil and you probably do not even recognize it. Just let me say quickly, you are being baited. Do not take this bait. They want you to see an enemy so that we turn on each other. Learn from the battles of the past. It takes two to play any game. In order to keep the game going you have to have two groups OPPOSING each other. Look closely over the past few years and you can see how they give us situations so that we chose a side. What you resists persists. The basic composition of EVERY problem in life is intention versus counter-intention. What you do not know is that they have to create an evil enemy that will unite humanity and we will work together, by doing that we will move into the next phase. Ironically, the only reason they have to do this is because we do not willingly come together and work as one human race. If we did, then they would not be permitted to carry out the Tribulation and Armageddon agenda.

If you are looking at these people as your enemies then you will begin to see enemies everywhere. As soon as you think that you need to protect yourself, you buy a weapon, then you will attract a situation that requires you to protect yourself, and you will be consumed by the battle. Now look closer at your everyday games and see where you and your friends are being setup.

First of all, take a look at all of the different video games on the market today. Depending on your personality type, the type of game you will pick up and play trains you. Whether it is a battle game where you learn battlefield strategies or city building games that teach you how to set up a structure of a city and take care of its people or go on a quest. We all know that the best games require you to register for them online. Guess what, you are being put into a classification on your training. All of these systems are linked. They will see how well you do in these training levels.

Next look at the similar techniques that bullies usc to force people into submission. Once you recognize these signs you can begin to use strategies that will enable you to gain the upper hand.

The first technique that they use is creating chaos around you. A bully will use every way possible to cause you to be confused. Because when we are in confusion, we stop moving our lives forward. These techniques are designed to divert your attention from what they are actually setting up behind your back to spring their "attack" on you. A common technique is to give you wrong reasons why things are happening. They release one side of the topic then spin the other side of that topic. Like what we have been seeing in the media.

As that information is filtering out to the masses you will see the public take one side or another. This duality is a deceptive practice from ancient battle strategies to divide and conquer them.

Behind the scenes what they are not coming out and saying to us is that they have to give us a warning of things to come. They will not be permitted to carry out this take over if we turn from our wicked ways. But depending on what religion you are looking at, there are many grey areas as to what our wicked ways actually are, I will break that down for you later in this book. Spoiler alert: it is not what we have been taught!

In the next chapter I will break down the Great Deception that these people have fallen for and I will show you how you will easily be able to see who took the real mark that God marked on Satan, and it is not a mark in your hand or forehead!

The next common technique that a bully can use is causing fear. Fear is the main emotion that is designed to make you stop in your tracks. Fear is what immobilizes humanity. It causes you not to move, so that your enemy can get you into position for their attack. In this real time agenda unfolding, they use propaganda to create confusion, so the greatest fear is fear of the unknown. Using our imagination against us. It is an ancient battle strategy using modern technology.

The next strategy is what is known as the "Forgetter Sequence." This is a series of confusing bits of information that will be in the form of a question, "What if this?" "What if that?" By giving you different fear-based scenarios, it causes us to forget what we were doing before that sequence started. When really the time leading up to the main event is the most critical to your victory!

So, whenever you are dealing with this kind of a set up cut that person's access to your survival quickly! Take this time to become independent and self sustainable as possible. It may take some time to get to the point that you can stand on your own two feet, you are better off disciplining yourself and doing what you need to in order to not allow them to gain access to the things you absolutely have to have in order to survive.

Then when you have got those things in place, just stand, and become the observer of their behavior. Obviously, you are not going to trust this person and as you are observing them you will see an action to take when it comes up. If you look back in your life you will notice that problems that you were trying to solve do not actually resolve until you get to the day that you suddenly will have that last piece of the puzzle and everything falls into place.

Being able to determine what decision to make is critical! Whether you are in a life-threatening moment or not, we will live the results of the decisions we make, good or bad. One wrong decision can throw your life into a tailspin in an instant that can take you years to dig your way out of, I still do not understand why we are not teaching this in school!

Do not allow your emotions to vote! This is how you can get a handle on them in an instant! Inhale slowly and put your attention on your breath. When you do this, in an instant your mind will be silent, and you will have your emotions in check, you will be clear headed and be able to see if there is an action for you to take. If you are dealing with a more drastic situation and you need to force your mind not to focus on what you are dealing with then give your brain other types of stimulus, such as touch, smell and so on. Put your hand in your pocket and put your attention on how the material feels. If you do not have pockets, then put your attention on how your shirt feels on your back. Can you feel the weight of it? Put your attention on your feet inside of your shoes. Are your socks soft? Are your feet cold or hot? Forcing your mind to focus on other things is especially important when dealing with people.

There is something I want to ask everyone, "If you really are a believer, and you believe in the kingdom that is to come, then why are you not focused on the finish line instead of the test?" Many other teachings have taught the power of visualization and focusing on what you want, not what you do not want. So, my point is that by reading, and broadcasting to everyone what the Tribulation is all about and the battle of Armageddon, you are giving more power to our enemy than he deserves! I get so sick of how these images of Satan show that he is this all powerful being when in the Bible it says that when we are brought in front of the Great White Throne for Judgment Day, we will all be amazed at this weak looking being that has held humanity captive for so long.

Get a grip on reality! Focus on where our goal is in this agenda! Set your sights on Heaven, praise our Heavenly Father, and welcome in the God of ALL Gods, the God of ALL creation! Welcome in the Most High God who created all living things! He created the Heavens and the Earth and everything in between! There are 365 "Fear Not's" in the Bible because we are going to need one for each day of the year! Breathe through the fear and walk through the fire. Allow these hard times to purify you. That is what the fire does, it burns out the impurities. We really do not have any other choice. Either the fire will refine you or it will consume you, it is your choice.

Chapter 5
Truth Behind the Secret Societies

Whether or not you are interested in the various conspiracy theories out there, it does not take a rocket scientist to see that there are secret societies involved within the major changes in our society throughout history. Honestly, if they all work together toward a common goal, things would change so quick it would make your head spin!

Although the common misunderstanding is the theory that these groups function as one organization. That just is not the reality of the situation. Much like what you see in Davos, there is a give and take among them with a lot of ego's going around.

Which is why this 'green' movement has taken so long to get off the ground. Trust me, if they cannot see a way to make money at it, then it will never fly!

On many different occasions in human history many of these types of revolutions were orchestrated where one order would be battling another order. The leaders of these orders were known members, so it was a case that they knew they were waging war with their sworn brothers in these brotherhoods.

A classic example is World War I. It was common that the elite would only mate with other 'blue blooded elite.' This caused a problem in WWI that these blue bloods were really fighting their cousins! In some battles it was a case where one Freemason

General was battling another Freemason General. This is the reason that in all fairness you cannot generalize that secret societies are one group against humanity. Even though there is a common theme of the haves against the have nots.

These groups are made up of 144 orders. There are 72 orders known as the Great White Brotherhood and 72 orders of the Great Dark Brotherhood. Fact is that the good and evil balance each other out. They keep each other in check. To everything there is a time and a place. These groups put humanity through hard times so that we pull together and work as one species, then they give us easy times, so we can relax.

In hard times in most cases throughout history, food and money are scarce, we learn ways to make every little resource stretch as long as possible. They make it look like it is a battle of good against evil so that we pick a side and see an enemy to battle.

Really what they are hiding is that by putting us through good times and bad, it causes us to evolve. We learn the most when we are living in the hard times. That is when we have to pull together and work as one race. Look back at your life, you grow in the hard times, you do not learn anything in the easy times. Those times are designed to give you a time out to recharge yourself and get ready for the next round.

To my understanding, there are cultures that have been taught that the only way that they will be welcomed into the 'new Earth' is by carrying out their evil task here first.

The crazy thing to me is that I can see both sides of the 'fence' that separates us. By these groups creating an especially evil monster for everyone to overcome, then the people who are choosing not to take a religious side they will end up making that choice when they are face to face with someone or something that threatens life. With the advancements of Artificial Intelligence many people think that we will face an evil thing to overcome. I do not rule that possibility out.

So, in that respect I can see the benefit in dealing with pure evil. It will make you turn from your wicked ways, like it or not.

By causing a food shortage and eliminating mankind's access to meat, then we will not be able to eat the meat of animals. Eating meat will keep you grounded. The Bible says that we will take up Wings as Eagles. If you were born with wings, then why do you choose to crawl? There is one common single dream that humanity dreams, that no one talks about. When we are young, we all have vivid dreams of flying. Depending on your age, you may still have those dreams. There is a reason for it.

There is a point that we will soon get to when we will remember who we are and what we are capable of doing. Our bodies are fearfully and wonderfully made. Most people do not remember how to tap into that power, yet. That day is coming.

We gain our greatest strengths in adversity. If the only time that humanity will work together is in a tragedy, then guess what God will continue to put us through? This is the real reason that man choses to suffer and this is how we make that choice. Even when you chose not to make a choice you have still picked a side. If everyone only did good, there would be little adversity to overcome.

And in case you did not catch what was happening before the release of this virus, humanity was getting bored with the easy times. So much so that we began to turn on each other and ourselves. More people were turning to suicides and drug overdoses. When you look at us as one species it really is funny how we go from one extreme to the other and cannot seem to be happy. We are hooked on our own misery.

Like I said earlier, these groups are working on a specific timeline, not just the 2033 agenda. The real thing that they are not talking about is that as we evolve, we will get to the point that we must literally be born again. Why? Because we have been like a baby in the womb, there are complications if the baby is born too early or too late. The baby must be born again at exactly 9 months.

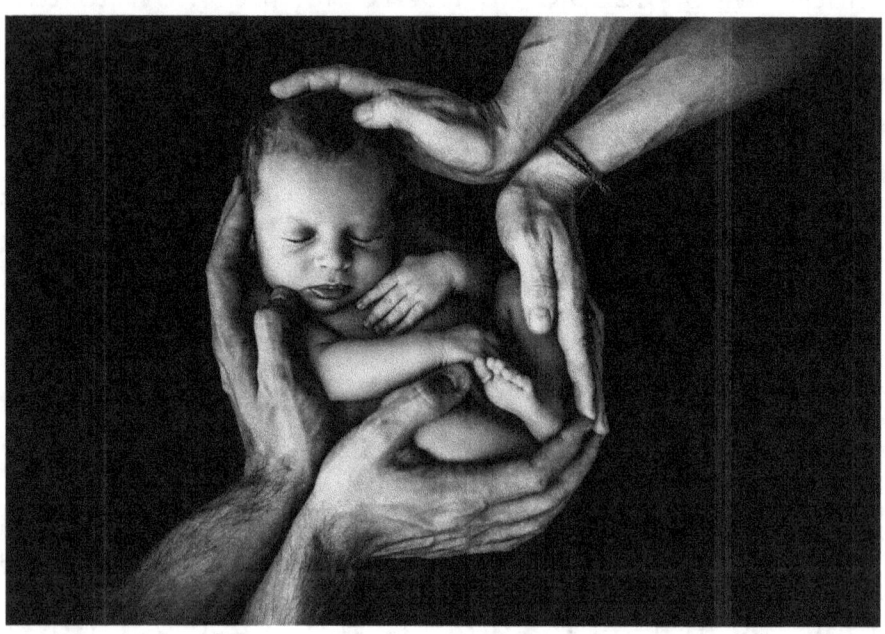

Since our fall, they have been teaching us and introducing greater technologies as "toys" for us to play with and learn from. Soon we will have acquired all of the knowledge that we were to learn here, at that point we will advance from here to the next phase. That is when we will enter Zion. That is the real agenda behind their plan in their 'population control' agenda. We were never meant to stay at this level.

By Blu Diamond

Chapter 6
How the Mighty Will Fall!

In the previous chapter I have shown you part of what these secret societies plan is for humanity. Now I will show you how Satan has been leading these groups into a trap. This comes from a very ancient deception that they do not even recognize as a lie. I guarantee to you that this is how they will be destroyed by God. As you will see we will dive deep in this one, so hang with me. Much of this has not been taught to the mainstream.

When you study these secret societies that have formed over the centuries, the major ones have the same theme. Ironically enough that theme is what they believe is a common thread of 'truth' in all of the major religions as well.

So, I am not going to name them, because it was common practice then and it still is common today that we automatically think that the oldest information has to be the right information on any subject. That has gotten humanity into trouble more than once.

In this case, that information has spawned a Great Deception that is trying to get in our faces today with the movement of these global leaders. This is their "inner circle's" main goal, on both sides of the fence. Whether or not the outer bands of these groups are aware of it, this is their target.

Let me begin to sketch this out for you. I think it is easiest to begin with the secret society that seems to have had the same publicist as Jesus himself. There is not a single person on the planet today that has not heard of the Illuminati. Just in case you have lived under a rock for the last forty years while they were advertising themselves and their plan for a New World Order, I will simplify this group and their real hidden agenda.

This group, like many others, have the common goal to create a new society of enlightened elite that will rule the world. In this past year, during COVID-19 many people have begun studying this group to try to figure out what to do about them.

The original group was founded in Ingolstadt, Bavaria by Adam Weishaupt. At the age of 15 he started his college career at the Jesuit college University of Ingolstadt. There he studied Canon

Law. He graduated in 1768 at age 20 and assumed a Professorship at the college. Later he would become the Deacon.

His plan was to create an organization that would make men free and happy, but first he had to make them 'good again.' That required his group to set man free of the chains that kept mankind down.

In his plan he saw that the kingdom that is to come in the Millennial reign of Christ or what the Jewish people saw with the coming of their Messiah would be instituted by humans themselves. In his mind that would begin with the illuminated elite leading the way. This world revolution would result in a one world republic that required the destruction of Christianity and all other forms of religion. And the annihilation of all governments. This would bring 'liberation' from all social, moral, and religious restraint. Look around at this post covid world, does it not look like this agenda is being carried out today?

In his mind, then mankind could embrace absolute equality and social fraternity. In his view religious superstition would be replaced with atheism for the masses and a kind of 'enlightened' Pantheism for the higher classes. This type of Pantheism in his plan is a doctrine that the universe, conceived as a whole is God, and conversely that there is no God but the combined substance, forces and laws that are manifested in the existing universe. (Note, there is still a 'higher class' there is no real equality.) They would initiate a kind of 'communism of goods' would govern economics. (Like the Davos agenda that we will own nothing and be "happy.") His group would be viewed as a "Benevolent Enlightened Elite" that would reign over this 'so called' paradise. (Sounding familiar?)

"The superiors of Illuminism are to be looked upon as the 'most perfect' and the 'most enlightened' of men. No doubts are to be entertained even of their infallibility." Adam Weishaupt.

"The great strength of our order lies in its concealment; let it never appear in its own name, but always covered by another name and another occupation." Adam Weishaupt.

His group began with five men who were incredibly involved with the 18th Century Enlightenment period. That movement in history is thought to be the 'Flowering of Reason and Science' but it also saw had an explosion of interest in Mysticism and the Occult.

The Freemasons call themselves the 'Initiates of the Flame.' Both of these groups claim to be "enlightened." The Illuminati joined the freemasons shortly after forming and had plans to position themselves into positions of power and influence within this organization.

Occult and Masonic scholar, and author of many books, Manly P. Hall (who was a Freemason) said that the Bavarian Illuminati were, "But a fragment of a much larger movement." He viewed Weishaupt as a faithful servant of a larger cause. And that behind him moved the intricate machinery of the Ancient Secret Mystery Schools. Hall warned that these Mystery Schools never trust their full weight to any perishable institutions. "The Bavarian Illuminati are but a chapter in a story, not the whole story." Manly P. Hall

Weishaupt said, "Of all the means I know to lead men, the most effectual is a concealed mystery. The hankering of the mind is irresistible.....In this time, when the games and abuses of secret societies were without end, I wanted to make use of this human weakness for a real and worthy goal, the welfare of mankind."

That much larger movement is what I will cover here. This movement has had the same message with the same theme across many religions. From everything that I have seen on it, it appears to have originated near 500 B.C., or at least that is the earliest records that Historians and Archaeologists can track.

Around 500 B.C. the Pythagorean Brotherhood appeared near Greece and Italy. This secret society is the earliest group that we know of that had roots in Gnostic beliefs.

This mystical society is where we can trace back the origins of Merkaba Mysticism. That is Ezekiel's visions of wheels within wheels. Also known as the Chariot of Fire that the Prophets Enoch and Elijah ascended in to enter the Heavens without dying. The Pythagorean Brotherhood is said to have practiced ascension which is this mysticism. They also practiced vegetarianism and initiated women.

The root of this theme comes from Gnosticism. Gnosticism believes that there are two Gods, also known as a dualist religion. A 'good' God and an 'evil' God. Gnosticism comes in many different religious traditions across the globe. There are Gnostic groups in Judaism, Egyptian, Greek, Pagan, Islamic and this is also the earliest Christian movement known in antiquity. This theme is taught in Hinduism, Buddhism, Sufism, Christianity, Islam, and many, many others!

The word Gnosis is Greek it means knowledge. Gnosticism believes that our path to ascend back to the celestial realm that we came from is through knowledge, not faith.

This is the "Path to Illumination" that has been passed on from generation to generation within these secret societies and many religions. And this is how it spread across regions and religions throughout human history. From the earliest records down through Plato, and Socrates to modern day Freemasons, Rosicrucian, and the illusive Illuminati and many, many others. As you can see there really is a thin veil separating these secret societies from religions on this planet.

The common theme is that we are 'divine' beings that are trapped in our physical bodies here, we are stuck in this cycle of reincarnating. These groups teach that we need to learn how to (ascend) in order to get to 'Heaven' through vegetarianism, and how to live and remembering who we are and how we got here.

Christianity and Islam teach that we are the fallen Angels that were tricked by Satan at his rebellion. We are trapped here and have to find our way back. Our goal as a species is to learn what we need to in order to ascend back to the celestial realm that we came from so that we will not reincarnate here again.

In the New Testament we are taught that we will get our 'glorified bodies.' Jesus taught that this path is offered to the Gentiles through doing the will of the Father and how to suffer. And Apostle Paul taught that only believing in the resurrection is our path to salvation and that we must die to get our 'Glorified Body.' No matter what you call it, the theme is the same.

I know this information from Christian teachings, and like I mentioned at the beginning of this book, when I was a little girl my Grandfather taught me about these groups. Although like many of you whose Grandparents may have been members of these groups, you know that these secret teachings are designed as an enigma.

After being raised as a Christian, God tested me for many years. My life went crazy, and I had to prove myself to the Father in Heaven. Then as I passed more and more levels of tests of my character, I finally got to a point that the Father began showing me the teachings of this Chariot of Fire.

Something in me kept telling me that something was not right. After being shown all of the teachings, then the Most High began showing me the Biblical connections. Making the connection through the scriptures, I then realized that He was showing me the Great Deception. I was deceived by it at first myself.

God has shown me much older teachings on what Jesus called the Baptism of Fire, also known as the Baptism of the Spirit. The word Baptism means 'change.' Even though in the Bible the path that Jesus taught was removed, there are still symbols of this path and subtle hints throughout the scriptures and religious symbology in the Abrahamic religions.

You see, this ancient path of activating this Chariot of Fire dates back to the Garden of Eden. In the center of the Garden of Eden there were two trees. The Tree of the Knowledge of Good and Evil (which God told Adam and Eve that if they ate from it, they would die. This is what happened that makes us reincarnate here over and over. This information used to be in the Bible but was removed in the 1500's) and the other tree was the Tree of Life.

I have been shown that this is why in Jewish traditions a young man training to become a Rabbi must study God's Laws first for many years as he is growing and learning then later in life, he is permitted at a certain age to study the Kabbalah. The ancient Hebrew language is a living language, those sounds are the real Tree of Life. Remember we speak things into existence.

If you do not have the proper training leading up to this then you will not have the whole picture on this path. Which is what I am afraid of with the elite. It does not appear that they have taken the time to study the whole picture. Which is why in the book of Revelation 13:10 'He that leadeth into captivity shall go into captivity: he that killeth with the sword must be killed with the sword. Here is the patience and the faith of the saints.'

The people who have taken this mark today become evil. Suddenly they have all of the esoteric knowledge. Much like what happened in the 'Age of Enlightenment.'

By taking this mark of that beast you are eating from the tree in the Garden of Eden known as the Tree of the Knowledge of Good and Evil. In my understanding, many people know that the teachings of the "Chariot of Fire' comes from the Kabbalah. Some people understand that the information contained in the Kabbalah comes from the Tree of the Knowledge of Good and Evil. This is the information that the Ancient Mystery Schools were founded upon.

At Satan's rebellion he wanted to find a way to be like God. He wanted to be loved and worshipped

The Great Reset Hidden Agenda

like God. And this is how he tricked ancient man during the 'Dark Ages' by telling them that they do not have to die, if they do this they will be like God. Even the ones that I saw in the field I was studying this Chariot of Fire started acting vastly different. The people I was with started calling themselves 'co-creators' and 'demi-gods.' And very strange things were happening to them.

I can go into many more scripture references but my goal here is not to highlight this mess because it is an ancient deception.

What everyone seems to have 'glossed over' is the fact that Satan is the Angel of light! The Heavenly Father, the God of all Creation had put a mark in the belly of Satan when he rebelled. This mark is a flame, that in the end times it will become an all-consuming fire to him and anyone who takes this mark will be consumed! If the elite have ignited this flame and truly have become "enlightened" then the fire that burns within them will consume them. In other words, this sparks spontaneous human combustion. This is what happened during the Great Fire of Rome! The spirit that came down from Heaven and appeared to the 500 and to Apostle Paul to "convert" him was the same spirit that took Jesus up on the mountain of God to be tempted by Satan.

57

Jesus fasted for 40 days and 40 nights to endure this temptation. The 500 and Apostle Paul did not fast and were not Baptized in Water just before that appearance. And what many people do not know is that the Baptism that the Disciples received happened approximately 27 years before this spirit appeared to Paul and the 500. Let me show you scripturally the real mark that God gave Satan. This is the real Mark of the Beast.

Ezekiel 28:13-19 KJV

13)"Thou hast been in Eden the garden of God; every precious stone was thy covering, the Sardius, Topaz, and the Diamond, the Beryl, the Onyx, and the Jasper, the Sapphire, the Emerald and the Carbuncle, and Gold; the workmanship of thy Tabrets and of thy pipes (his body was made of musical instruments and jewels) was prepared in thee in the day that thou was created.

14) Thou art the anointed cherub that covereth; and I have set thee so: thou was upon the holy mountain of God: thou hast walked up and down in the midst of the stones of fire. 15) Thou was perfect in thy ways from the day that thou was created, till iniquity was found in thee. 16) By the multitude of thy merchandise they have filled the midst of thee with violence, and thou hast sinned: therefore, I will cast thee as profane out of the mountain of God:

and I will destroy thee, O covering cherub, from the midst of the stones of fire. 17) Thine heart was lifted up because of thy beauty, thou hast corrupted thy wisdom by reason of thy brightness (this proves he is an Angel of light; the path of light is evil): I will cast thee to the ground, I will lay thee before Kings, that they may behold thee. 18) Thou hast defiled thy sanctuaries by the multitude of thine iniquities, by the iniquity of thy traffic; therefore, will I bring forth a fire from the midst of thee, it shall devour thee, and I will bring thee to ashes upon the earth in the sight of all of them that behold thee. 19) All they that know thee among the people shall be astonished at thee: thou shalt be a terror, and never shalt thou be any more."

You can clearly see that the real way that God marked Satan is with a flame in his belly, and that flame will become an all-consuming fire when he is laid in front of the Kings of the Earth.

If these current Kings have taken this mark of this beast, they will be destroyed with him. This is the real mark that we should not take. That flame activates this Chariot of Fire, also known as the Baptism of the Spirit, that 'illuminates' you and connects you with a 'divine realm' that is evil.

When God created Adam, God called the Angels to Him and commanded them to bow down to His creation. All of them did except Satan. Satan perceived this as God loving man more than Satan.

We just have to make the right decisions right now and get this right! And as you can see from the earlier verses in Ezekiel 28 that Satan was His beloved Angel. Satan was jealous and refused to bow. His great plan was to deceive God's creation and lead us astray so that we commit the ultimate sin by turning away from our Heavenly Father and worshipping Satan. This is the true history that I can prove of how Satan has carried out that plan during the dark ages which was mankind's weakest moment.

These religions and secret societies that follow this 'path to illumination' are in more trouble than they realize.

In Adam Weishaupt own words, "The most wonderful thing of all.... Is that the distinguished Lutheran and Calvinist theologians who belong to our order really believe that they see in the Illuminati the true and genuine sense of the Christian religion. Oh, mortal man, is there nothing you cannot be made to believe?"

In the classic era any initiate into a mystery cult was called and still are called an illuminatus, this is the same term that was used for a Christian who had also undergone this Baptism of Fire. The

Roman emperor Nero blamed the Christians for the Great Fire of Rome, now I believe him. The reason for the Christian crusades were not what we have been taught. One Roman historian wrote about this phenomenon that came from Judea and was spreading across Rome was an abomination to humanity. That is the same point of view that Apostle Paul had before that demon appeared to him and "converted" him. Mark my words, this is how the elite class will be destroyed.

By Blu Diamond

Chapter 7
Man Plans His Ways but God Directs His Steps!

Our Heavenly Father has created a perfect crucible. This situation that we find ourselves in is unprecedented. The decisions we make this year alone can spin our existence into a place of beauty or a place of utter destruction, and not just by us destroying ourselves as you can see.

The urgent issues that these global leaders have brought to our attention do need to be addressed, but we do not have to perish to fix it. Obviously, the way that these corporations have destroyed ecosystems to create the products that they market to the masses, needs to change. And how we process waste needs to be upgraded. This will require all hands-on deck, working as one.

What the working class does not know is that the elite have already been told that they cannot get to the new Earth (Zion, what some people call Heaven) without us. You see, they do not have the ability to love. In order to love completely, you have to have the ability to put yourself in other people's shoes and feel how these situations would make you feel then change your actions accordingly. That is a skill that many need to develop called empathy.

This is why earlier in this book; I commended the work that Klaus Schwab is starting, to a point. Much like the Yin and Yang symbol there is a bit of darkness in the light and light in the darkness. Nothing is pure on either side. He is making these leaders come to the table with peer pressure to be held accountable to create solutions for all.

At least he is making the effort, and if we can reign in this beast we can travel through this safely. These groups know that if they do not support us during this transition that we will destroy everything in sight.

Chapter 8
What the Elite Really Fear

Let me show you the power of the Most High in your own life and you probably did not even recognize His hand at work. Have you ever been doing something that you knew you were not supposed to be doing, and pretty soon you start getting consequences for that action?

If you notice, each time you go back to doing that thing that you are not supposed to be doing, those consequences get harder and harder until suddenly your life will shift, and you can no longer do what you were doing. That is the power of the Most High, He is chastising you. In the Bible He says that He only chastises the sons and daughters that He is planning on taking into Heaven. So, if everyone is getting that correction then why are we taught that anyone will be left behind?

The Most High is positioning us for that day known as the Great and Terrible Day of the Lord. That is the day that we will see the Sun go black for more than 2 hours, that is the normal length of time for an eclipse. If the Sun stays black, then you have a total of 5 hours from the beginning of that eclipse to get into an Earth based structure.

The indigenous tribes on the planet know this and they have been waiting for that day for almost 2000 years now. The Bible says that the meek will inherit the Earth. This is the real day that these secret societies fear the most. This is the day that they want us to save them from. I can go into greater detail about this situation that will really blow your mind, but instead of giving you things that you would not understand, let me just give you what you need to know.

When you are looking for an Earth based structure, it has to be made purely of Earth, absolutely no synthetic material. Like a cave. The Native Americans teach that this day is when the Earth will enter into the Great Void. That is the birth canal. This is the visions that Apostle Paul and Jesus had when they were teaching that we must be born again. This is the real way that the Earth will go from the age of Pisces to the age of Aquarius. Where there will be no more death. Where the Lion will lay down with the Lamb. This is known as the New Earth that God made called Zion. This is the real way that God had planned to redeem all bloodlines. God knows that we have sinned and because of our flesh we have a sinful nature that is nearly impossible to overcome while we are here. Apostle Paul and Jesus both taught that in the blink of an eye we will all die in corruption and be raised incorruptible. These teachings is why these groups are planning to eliminate two thirds of the population of the Earth.

The Earth has done this before, this is how we know what is about to take place. The ancient writings on cave walls in different tribal lands tells this story from the past. From the Dogon tribes to the Sumerians these Earth events have been recorded.

These people drew pictures to convey the message to any human that would come here after them, because there can be a language barrier. We know that the last time the Earth did this, the Sun was black for 2 ½ days. On that day what will really take place is a literal pole shift. When that pole shift happens, our spirits will be caught up and brought up into that celestial realm that we are from. In God's eyes we will be washed clean. This is why the Dinosaurs were walking along chewing their food and suddenly dropped dead. My plan is to make sure that Hell is empty of humans! My message to these Secret Societies is, "This is your Get out of Hell Free card! Use it! God had a plan all along to redeem all bloodlines!"

This is literally a human evolution. This is how previous humanoid species left here. Everything on the planet will gct a new body! Our old body goes away, and we are given a new body. So, if you are seeing God delaying you, or moving in your life, then you are going to be called up!

The Bible says that God only chastises the Sons and Daughters that He is planning on taking into

Heaven! Pay close attention to His Holy Spirit guiding you. It can be that type of correction in your life, or He will delay you to protect you from harm, or He will pave His loving grace before you and everything that you are doing will have an ease to it.

God does not speak in an audible voice; I have heard Him call my name once. Ever since then I watch my surroundings. God shows you signs around you to pay attention to. For example, if you are doing something wrong you will start seeing police cars everywhere. So, stop what you are doing! Change your direction, change your evil ways, figure out a different way. Many times, I have noticed that it can be a matter of timing. If I am still supposed to do that thing, then it might not be the right time yet. God is still working in the background setting things up. Everything in this universe happens at God's perfect timing. He is never early by our standards, but He is NEVER late either!

When you need God to help you with something, do not pray and ask, because our minds can limit the possibilities. Just start praising and thanking Him for taking care of it for you! This is the most powerful thing I can ever show you!

If you step out in radical obedience and only depend on Him, He will take care of your every need! You do not have to ask! Just praise Him, I sing to Him. He is our Father, and He wants to spend time with us! Set aside time in your day to just thank Him. Without Him we could not breathe! He gave us our breath!

And I can prove it to you! Place your hands palm facing palm with your fingers spread apart, inhale slowly and put your attention on the space in between your hands as you exhale slowly. Each time you inhale, and exhale try to slow down the breath to about 5 seconds in and out. Do not pause at the top of the breath or at the bottom. The space in between your hands will heat up! That is the breath of God that He breathed into your nostrils when He created you! Within the first year of a baby's life, you may have noticed the top of their head and the Perinium moving in and out when they breathe this is known as the Prana tube. It is the old way that we used to breathe. Our body takes in life source from our environment around us. That heat between your hands is that breath that God breathed into Adam's nostrils and this is proof that He created us in that same manner. Soon you will remember how to breathe, and we will leave this way of living behind us forever.

By Blu Diamond

Chapter 9
Secret Behind Davos Agenda

The biggest part of the World Economic Forums' plan of the 4th Industrial Revolution is the newest technologies that are being rolled out.

So, let me show you where they got these ideas, and why they are trying to use the original design to their economic advantage.

The real reason these plans are being rolled out is because a man by the name of Jacques Fresco dedicated his whole life in trying to create a smarter design for a society and smart cities. His finished plans would repair the damage to the environment within ten years. Which is the point of no return that we all must face.

His plans are laid out in Venus, Florida on 20 acres of land. It is called the Venus Project. He said before he died that he figured that just before the Earth was completely destroyed that is when the people would then build his design. And he was right, we played around ignoring the problem and now we do not have a choice. Please check out their website at www.thevenusproject.com (Image is Jacques Fresco Venus Project smart city design.)

With his building designs and city layouts it minimizes the amount of resources that a city uses. Although he warned that the only way that this design would work to eliminate crime and scarcity is if the working class built it with absolutely no currency exchange of any kind. No one would have to buy or sell anything. (Sound familiar?)

That is the only way to eliminate crime, this eliminates poverty. Most crime is done because of scarcity and lack. If we are made to believe that there is a shortage of something, then it becomes rare to us, and we place more value on that thing. The scarcity makes it more desirable to those who do not have it. It is what our system today is all about, the battle between the haves and the have nots.

In 2016 before his death, he was given an award by the United Nations for his city design. Since that was the only real plan that anyone had come up with to restore the damage to the Earth within ten years, then the elite took those plans and have figured up what they want to use out of it and what they want to discard. Obviously no global corporation or government is going to give up their system to make money. So, this has been the debate behind closed doors since 2016. This is the plan of the real Davos agenda. Which helps them create a new world.

The way I see it, we can either sit around and do nothing as they continue to advance the technology, then when they do roll this out, we will all have to deal with the desperate people who will be breaking into everything in sight to rob, steal and destroy. Or we can pull together and create a different option. Most people could not imagine living without technology, this is why more people are not wanting to farm for a living anymore. The way I see it is that we have two choices. One is high tech and the other is low tech. The high tech one is to group fund and build the Venus Project after all we are the working class; we have the skills and ability to beat them at their own game. Or the low-tech version is to pull together into Intentional Communities and eco communities. Both versions will embrace the hard to love people that are struggling. But as far as I can see, only the high-tech version of the Venus Project will give us the technology to battle the technology of the groups that are planning global domination. In my opinion we need action now because these people are moving quickly. And the more good people who get educated and involved with the technology then the good side will be able to catch when the bad side is trying to pull something underhanded. There has to be a balance in life.

Now you can see this problem through my eyes. Humanity we have painted ourselves into the enigma of the Illumined one's plans. Afterall we would not have it any other way. We thrive in doing the impossible!

If we continue to ignore the problem, we will destroy the earth and all of its resources that we need to live. If we wait, we will deal with mass starvation and the Great Famine. If we follow what Jesus taught, that was to eliminate poverty, illness, and death, then the closest we can come is the Venus Project, it eliminates two out of three, without taking any mark of the beast, either with currency to buy and sell or with the internal flame. In reality, these noble religions are right about one main thing, it is our love of money that keeps us in prison. The elite refuse to give up their control of the money, the working class is trapped in the hamster wheel of working to survive and our kids get angry because we are never home to spend time with them. In reality, building a massive city design project will only happen in a few places at best without tearing down those current city structures, some of which have gone without upkeep for so long that they need to be rebuilt anyway.

My message to the current generations on the planet today. We have one shot at this, you have all been wondering what this life is all about, why are we here. There has never been a greater, more noble cause than the task at hand. This is going to require looking past borders, and skin color, past pain from one ethnicity to another. Your parents should have taught you to share, now more than ever you need to see that the time of selfishness is over. It has to be over if your children and grandchildren will survive.

As you look into their eyes, how can you say to them that when we had the chance to make it right, we did nothing like the generations before us. That type of complacency and passing the buck behavior needs to be put behind us with all of the pain and separation that it has caused.

I look at all of you as my sisters and brothers no matter where you come from and what your religious beliefs are, we all bleed red. We are one race, Mankind. Now pull yourself up by the bootstraps and let's get busy cleaning this place up! I love you all and I have faith in our ability to fix this without violence and bloodshed. But if it is going to happen, we have to act now!

Forever in Service,
Blu Diamond
P.S. Remember, Diamonds are created under extreme amounts of pressure. That is why this life is so hard. This will make you come out shinning!

About the Author

My name is Carol Farley, I write under the penname of Blu Diamond so that my books are not confused by a previous author by the same name. (Honestly, it is my name too!)

Everyone across North America know me by Blu Diamond. I travel coast to coast and Canada. Diamonds are created under extreme amounts of pressure, that is why this is called a School of Hard Knocks. Every religion says that we are not from here, and that we are not staying!

I have been guided to learn the ancient teachings from antiquity that will light our path home. My plan is to teach as many people as I can before I leave here.

Check out my author website www.bludiamond.org and subscribe to my main teaching website www.universalmizfitz.com We are all mizfitz here!

79

By Blu Diamond

www.ingramcontent.com/pod-product-compliance
Lightning Source LLC
Chambersburg PA
CBHW071027220526
45467CB00004B/1541